"The writ
live the g
— James Cardinal Hickey

"Mrs. Doherty's books are always best sellers and with good reason. Her writing is clear, to the point, so that it is hard to miss what she is saying."

— *The Crux of Prayer*

"Reading Catherine Doherty's writings has always been both a pleasure and an enriching experience."

— *Spirituality Today*

"Catherine Doherty's years of total dedication to the people of God, the crosses she has carried, and the tremendous graces she has received all leave their mark on what she writes, adding new depths now to the perception which has always been hers. . . . a present-day prophet whose commission is validated by a long life spent in 'living the Gospel without compromise.'"

— *Sisters Today*

"Catherine Doherty has the gift of a great and joyous faith and of making life an adventure, a pilgrimage."

— Dorothy Day

God in the
Nitty-Gritty Life

Snippets from the writings of

Catherine de Hueck Doherty

MADONNA HOUSE PUBLICATIONS
Combermere, Ontario, Canada

Madonna House Publications®
2888 Dafoe Rd
Combermere ON K0J 1L0

www.madonnahouse.org/publications

First Edition

First printing, June 8, 2002 — feast of the Immaculate Heart

Printed in Canada

Compiled by Miriam Stulberg

Scripture quotations are taken from the Jerusalem Bible, copyright © 1969 by Darton, Longman & Todd, London.

National Library of Canada Cataloguing in Publication Data

Doherty, Catherine de Hueck (née Kolyschkine), 1896–1985
    God in the nitty-gritty life

ISBN 0-921440-82-0

    1. Christian life. I. Title.

BX2350.D63 2002   248   C2002-902824-8

Design by Rob Huston

This book is set in Berkeley Oldstyle, designed by Frederic W. Goudy for the University of California Press in 1938. Headings are set in Caliban, designed by America's famous carver of inscriptions, John Benson, by writing with a blunt-point pen on rough paper.

The following excerpts are meant to be read slowly, one by one, or opened to at random.

Meditate on them, together with the accompanying scripture quotation, and let them open to you a new facet of gospel living. Taken as a whole, they will give you an overview of Catherine Doherty's spirituality.

Contents

Global warming

Because people do not love, the world is a very cold place. There is lust. There is temporary commitment to what appears to be love. But real love is something else entirely.

Love is God. Love is a Person. Love is stronger than death. The heart of God calls us to give him our heart, which means to give him ourselves. We must hold nothing back. It is by loving God in the nitty-gritty routine of our daily life that we make up for the coldness of other hearts.

"All that came to be had life in him and that life was the light of men, the light that shines in the dark, a light that darkness could not overpower."

– John 1:4–5 –

The bottom line

The greatest tragedy of our world is that we do not know that God loves us. Consequently, we do not know how to love him in return. Even Christians do not realize that our faith, in essence, is a passionate love affair between God and each human being. God so loved each one of us that he created us in his image. He so loved each of us that he became human himself, died on a cross, was raised from the dead, and ascended into heaven in order to bring each of us back to himself, to the divine life we had lost through original sin.

Christianity has its rules and dogmas, of course, but ultimately, they all have to do with love. God is love, and where love is, God is.

"Out of his infinite glory, may he give you the power through his Spirit for your hidden self to grow strong, so that Christ may live in your hearts through faith, and then, planted in love

and built on love, you will with all the saints have strength to grasp the breadth and the length, the height and the depth; until, knowing the love of Christ, which is beyond all knowledge, you are filled with the utter fullness of God."

— Ephesians 3:16–19 —

From start to finish

Faith is not a matter of attending the liturgy on Sundays. Living the Christian faith is a way of life that embraces every minute of our waking hours, and which permeates our whole life, whether at work or at home, at school or at play, from the cradle to the grave.

Once we understand this, a change will take place in our hearts, and the ultimate goal of our life will be clear. We shall realize that we have been created to love. We shall understand that all vocations, including marriage, are vocations to love.

"You did not choose me, no, I chose you and I commissioned you to go out and to bear fruit, fruit that will last."

– John 15:16 –

Identity

No matter who I am—single or married, young or old, man or woman, priest, nun or lay person—I should give God my whole self. I belong to him because he created me. He has full power over my life and my death. It is not out of fear that I should surrender, but from a passionate love for him who gave himself so passionately for me. Then I will enter into his resurrection, and he will continue to reveal his mysteries to me, slowly and gently, and the Holy Spirit will explain to me anything I do not understand.

"Make your home in me, as I make mine in you. As a branch cannot bear fruit all by itself, but must remain part of the vine, neither can you unless you remain in me."

– John 15:4 –

Facing him

Faith is a gift of God. Only he can bestow it, and it is a gift that he passionately desires to give us. However, he can only give it to us if we ask for it.

When we ask for faith, we are turning our face towards his face, and he can look into our heart. He loves to see us facing him, but we for some reason try to avoid this. Even while begging him for favors, we close the eyes of our soul, so as to avoid looking at him. Yet he is always looking at us, with deep love.

It is faith that allows us to enter peacefully into the dark night each of us faces at one time or another. Faith walks simply, like a child, between the darkness of human life and the hope of what is to come, "for eye has not seen, nor ear heard what God reserves for those who love him." Faith is a kind of folly, a folly of God himself.

Faith breaks through barriers. When our face is turned to God in faith, our eyes meet his, and each day becomes more luminous. The veil between God and us becomes thinner and thinner, until it seems we can almost reach out and touch him.

"For I am certain of this: neither death nor life, no angel, no prince, nothing that exists, nothing still to come, not any power, or height or depth, nor any created thing, can ever come between us and the love of God made visible in Christ Jesus our Lord."

~ Romans 8:38–39 ~

Empty cups

To be before God means to remember who God is.

It means knowing that we are empty cups that he must fill each day.

"The tax collector stood some distance away, not daring even to raise his eyes to heaven; but he beat his breast and said, 'God, be merciful to me, a sinner.'"

~ Luke 18:14 ~

A key

We crave greatness for our lives, but God asks us to become little. To pass through the door that leads to the Kingdom, we must go down on our knees.

"Anyone who wants to be great among you must be your servant, and anyone who wants to be first among you must be your slave, just as the Son of Man came not be served but to serve, and to give his life as a ransom for many."

— Matthew 20:27–28 —

Beggars and Princes

True humility comes from realizing who we are. We are created by God, creatures totally dependent on him. We are the poor people of God, the little ones who know that without him, they can do nothing.

This is the beginning of prayer. Cleansing ourselves of arrogance and pride, we come as beggars before Christ, who alone can make us princes and princesses, kings and queens, not of earthly kingdoms, but of the Kingdom of God.

When we are poor in this way, we can go to Bethlehem and meet the Child who became poor for us.

"I bless you, Father, Lord of heaven and of earth, for hiding these things from the learned and the clever and revealing them to mere children."

― Matthew 11:25 ―

Meeting

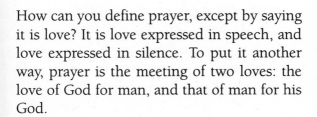

How can you define prayer, except by saying it is love? It is love expressed in speech, and love expressed in silence. To put it another way, prayer is the meeting of two loves: the love of God for man, and that of man for his God.

"We ourselves have known and put our faith in God's love towards ourselves. God is love and anyone who lives in love lives in God, and God in him."

~ 1 John 4:16 ~

Don't miss the boat!

The world today needs saints—hundreds, thousands, and millions of saints! Hate, fear, despair vanish like mist in the sun before men and women in love with God, men and women of sanctity.

Sanctity comes from much loving. For this we have been created: to love our neighbor, and through him, to love God. Loving is fun. Loving is joy. Loving brings peace. Loving means serving and forgetting oneself for others. Learn how to love and you will receive everything you need.

We are all called to be saints. Not to be a saint is the greatest tragedy that can befall a Christian today!

"You are God's chosen race, his saints; he loves you, and you should be clothed in sincere compassion, in kindness and humility, gentleness and patience. Bear with one another; forgive each other as soon as a quarrel beings. The Lord has forgiven you; now you must do the same.

Over all these clothes, to keep them together and complete them, put on love."

— Colossians 3:12–15 —

Gently

Christ told us to love our neighbor as ourselves. If you can't love yourself, you can't love anyone else. How important it is to be gentle with oneself!

We so often flagellate ourselves, dwelling on our sins and thinking we are horrible people. We harass ourselves, thinking of the wrong decisions we have made and the sins we have committed. We wound ourselves unceasingly, and we exhaust ourselves in the process.

We forget that the gentleness of God is part of his mercy. We forget that if we but turn to him and say, "I'm sorry", the sin is erased completely. He does not remember the sin. His mercy overshadows all.

How do you learn to be gentle? St. John used to recline on the breast of Christ. I think we will become gentle with ourselves and others if we do likewise. Then we will hear the heartbeats of God, and we will be able to help others hear them.

"Come to me, all you who labour and are over-burdened, and I will give you rest. Shoulder my yoke and learn from me, for I am gentle and humble in heart, and you will find rest for your souls."

- Matthew 11:28–29 -

Being in love

A young man and woman are in love. They want to get married. But do they love? Do they understand that the vocation of marriage is to love so well that their children will learn from them what love means?

Do they understand that marriage means self-surrender in love: love for one another and love for God? For love is neither selfish nor self-centered. Love never uses the pronoun "I".

"Love is always patient and kind; it is never jealous; love is never boastful or conceited; it is never rude or selfish; it does not take offence, and is not resentful. Love takes no pleasure in other people's sins but delights in the truth; it is always ready to excuse, to trust, to hope, and to endure whatever comes."

– 1 Corinthians 13:4–7 –

Sex

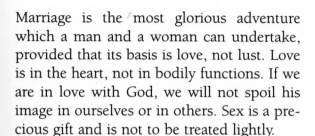

Marriage is the most glorious adventure which a man and a woman can undertake, provided that its basis is love, not lust. Love is in the heart, not in bodily functions. If we are in love with God, we will not spoil his image in ourselves or in others. Sex is a precious gift and is not to be treated lightly.

"Your body, you know, is the temple of the Holy Spirit, who is in you since you received him from God. You are not your own property; you have been bought and paid for. That is why you should use your body for the glory of God."

– 1 Corinthians 6:19–20 –

Deepest yearning

It is at Communion that husband and wife become one in the heart of Christ. The oneness is felt by those who believe, and in believing, see. It is here that the veil of faith becomes gossamer thin.

"Husbands should love their wives just as Christ loved the Church and sacrificed himself for her to make her holy.... In the same way, husbands must love their wives as they love their own bodies; for a man to love his wife is for him to love himself. A man never hates his own body, but he feeds it and looks after it; and that is the way Christ treats the Church, because it is his body—and we are its living parts."

— Ephesians 25:28–29 —

Centering

The Mass is our rendezvous with God. It is the place where we and Christ become one in the reality of faith. The Mass is the food that will sustain us as we ride the treadmill of one gray day after another. The love of Christ, given to us in the Eucharist, frees us from our chains. It is our strength, for he has said, "Without Me, you can do nothing."

When the priest says, "The Mass is ended, go in peace", we are reminded that the Lord calls us to live the Mass in the marketplaces of the world.

"Father…with me in them and you in me, may they be so completely one that the world will realize that it was you who sent me."

– John 17:23 –

How to keep going

Your life as a layperson in the world is hard. Around you, things may be grim, even sordid, but God will give you strength. Anything can be borne between two Masses. When you eat the Bread of Heaven, you will be able to face any kind of day. Your mind and heart will be nourished by the Word of God, the words of the psalmist. The warm voice of Christ will give you courage and new hope, and your faith will be renewed. You will plunge into the sea of fire that is the Mass, and you will come out burning, ready to go forth and kindle new flames of love.

Slowly, imperceptibly, the Mass brings us closer and closer to God and to Our Lady. It teaches us silence. With time, we will realize that within us is a hidden garden, and we have the key to its gate. We can enter there and meet our tremendous Lover. God loved us first, and all we have to do, as believers, is to love him in return.

"Father, I want those you have given me to be with me where I am, so that they may always see the glory you have given me…I have made your name known to them and will continue to make it known, so that the love with which you loved me may be in them, and so that I may be in them."

Connections

The secret of daily living is to connect an ordinary, seemingly boring life, in all its repetitive details, with Love, who is God. Then a day at the computer, when your back is aching and your mind reeling with tiredness, is a day that has redeemed many souls.

Christ is waiting for you to become aware of him, and of the work he has given you to do, by becoming aware of the connection between brooms, dishwater, laundry, cleaning, and the restoration of the world.

"Whatever you are doing, whether you speak or act, do everything in the name of the Lord Jesus, giving thanks to God the Father through him."

– Colossians 3:17 –

Fruit of monotony

Doing little things exceedingly well for the love of God, over and over again, is going to make you a saint. It is absolutely certain.

"The greatest among you must be your servant. Anyone who exalts himself will be humbled, and anyone who humbles himself will be exalted."

− Matthew 23:11–12 −

Connections 2

Everything in the world is touched by God. The chalice and host are visible signs of his presence, but to the eyes of faith, other objects are also signs. The vehicles we drive, the machines and appliances we use, also transmit God's creative intelligence working through the intelligence and creativity of men and women.

It follows, therefore, that whenever we misuse a tool, we desecrate something that has been co-created with God. This means we should recollect ourselves and think ahead before we even touch a button, or connect a plug.

When we take out our frustrations or hostilities on these products of God's collaboration with humanity, we only hurt ourselves. It is nearly as bad to manhandle a machine as it is to kick a dog. It is better to have the courage and humility to say, "I am upset today. It is better that I don't do this task," than to challenge the Lord by abusing his creation.

"Well done, good and faithful servant; you have shown you can be faithful in small things, I will trust you with greater; come and join in your master's happiness."

— Matthew 25:21 —

Witessing

How do you show the face of Christ? By doing what he asks you, one moment at a time. When you do the duty of the moment, you do something for Christ. You make a home for him in the place where your family dwells. You feed him when you feed your family. You wash his clothes when you do their laundry.

You help him in a hundred ways as a parent. Then the time will come when you will appear before him, and Christ will say to you, "I was hungry and you gave me to eat. I was thirsty, and you gave me to drink. I was sick and you looked after me."

"There were some women watching from a distance. Among them were Mary of Magdala, Mary who was the mother of James the younger, and Joset, and Salome. These used to follow him and look after him when he was in Galilee."

− Mark 15:40 −

"Come as you are"

Hospitality of the heart means accepting others as they are, not as we would like them to be, and allowing them to make themselves at home in one's heart. To be at home in another person's heart is to touch love. It is through the love of our brothers and sisters in Christ that we begin to understand the love of God.

"Be compassionate as your Father is compassionate. Do not judge, and you will not be judged yourselves; do not condemn, and you will not be condemned yourselves; grant pardon, and you will be pardoned."

— Luke 6:36–37 —

Almsgiving

Not everyone can give alms in money, but we all can give alms in words.

Alms of warm, kind words are like a mother's lullaby to the elderly, who have a kind of hungry loneliness. These words bring peace and joy to those who are sad and anxious, and make the unwanted feel loved and needed once more.

Do you see that child? Have you an extra moment to speak to him? Befriending a lonely or unloved child, be he rich or poor, is to bring Christ to that little one. Take the child into your heart. You will be taking Christ into your heart, and surely, in eternity, He will reverse the process!

"For I was hungry and you gave me food; I was thirsty and you gave me drink; I was a stranger and you made me welcome; naked and you clothed me, sick and you visited me, in prison and you came to see me."

~ Matthew 25:35-36 ~

Challenges

Let each day be a day of beginning again, of loving God a little more, of hungering for him a little more, of turning your face to him anew.

There is only one way to love God, and that is by loving your neighbor—the person next to you at any given moment. I repeat, turning your heart to Christ simply means turning to the one next to you.

Never forget: you shall be judged by love alone.

"My children, our love is not to be just words or mere talk, but something real and active; only by this can we be certain that we are children of the truth."

− 1 John 3:18–19 −

Connections 3

Where did I learn to connect physical things with spiritual truths? My parents never let me forget that every task, however ordinary, is of redeeming supernatural value, if done out of love.

Awareness of little things done well for the love of God is daily living lifted up into the heart of Christ. It means we rise in the morning, aware that this day is given to us so that we may grow in grace and wisdom before the Lord. It means that we have been given another day to spend in the school of God's love.

In order to enter heaven, we must be lovers. For instance, we wash the dishes for love of God. When you serve your family, do it quietly and efficiently. If you learn to connect serving to prayer, you will grow in wisdom and love, and you will become a light shining in the darkness of the world. This light from your loving service will lead people to God.

"It is not those who say to me, 'Lord, Lord,' who will enter the kingdom of heaven, but the person who does the will of my Father in heaven."

— Matthew 7:21 —

Pointers

No part of the Gospel is abstract. Each line cries out to be incarnated. Spirituality must become incarnate, just as Jesus Christ was incarnate.

Let me illustrate some ways to do this:

Be constantly watchful for the needs and pleasures of others, especially in little things.

Desire not to be loved but to love; not to be understood, but to understand.

Be careful not to let your anxiety, fear, irritation or moods darken the souls of others.

Apply good manners to daily living. For example, don't monopolize conversations.

Trust others. This is an important aspect of love, for love never judges another person. None of us "knows it all."

Don't confuse love with feelings. Love is not sentimental. Love knows when to say no.

"Everyone who listens to these words of mine and acts on them...will be like a sensible man who built his house on rock. Rain came down, floods rose, gales blew and hurled themselves against that house, and it did not fall."

— Matthew 7:24–25 —

About manners

Manners are "children of charity," and attention to these "little things" is the essence of living out our faith. Their infraction may seem to be only a scratch on the body of charity, but keep scratching, and you will soon have an open wound. We will not teach anyone to love if we behave thoughtlessly. How much harm can be done by lack of good manners!

"Do not speak harshly to a man older than yourself, but advise him as you would your own father; treat the younger men as brothers and older women as you would your mother. Always treat young women with propriety, as if they were sisters."

~ 1 Timothy 5:1–2 ~

A new look at food

Our Lady sanctified the kitchen when she transformed the fruits of the earth into nourishment for Christ's human body. Food became holy when he used ordinary bread and wine to feed us with himself. It was at a meal that he instituted the sacrament of the Eucharist. Throughout the ages, meals have been associated with hospitality and sharing, but ever since the Last Supper, the "breaking of the bread" has become a holy as well as a joyous occasion.

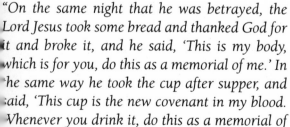

"On the same night that he was betrayed, the Lord Jesus took some bread and thanked God for it and broke it, and he said, 'This is my body, which is for you, do this as a memorial of me.' In the same way he took the cup after supper, and said, 'This cup is the new covenant in my blood. Whenever you drink it, do this as a memorial of me.'"

— 1 Corinthians 11:24–25 —

Potato peels and other things

I think of you working in the kitchen, peeling potatoes with great love of God as your duty of the moment. Suddenly the peelings are transformed into threads of silver and gold, reaching up to heaven and glorifying God. The angels, gently and reverently, wind up these threads, weaving from them a carpet for Our Lady's feet. I see this with the eyes of my soul, and I understand that the beauty of the threads depends on the intention of your heart. You have the power not only to turn dross into gold, but to turn gold back into dross.

On what depends the beauty of the threads? Charity. Charity in thought and charity in speech. It also depends on understanding, patience, and lack of envy.

To some people God gives great graces and opportunities. But you have a hidden life, a life of small things through which you can come to God in a little way, like St Therese of Lisieux. Others may do big things, but their temptations are great, and part of their reward is often already obtained on this earth. Not so with you. If you walk your way of littleness, your reward will be great in heaven.

"The kingdom of heaven is like a mustard seed which a man took and sowed in his field. It is the smallest of all the seeds, but when it has grown it is the biggest shrub of all and becomes a tree so that the birds of the air come and shelter in its branches."

— Matthew 13:31–32 —

Mary

You go to Jesus through his Mother. She possesses the secret of prayer and wisdom, for she is the Mother of God. Who else can teach you to burn with love, but the Mother of Love? Who else can teach you to pray, but the Woman of prayer? Who else can teach you to go into the silence of deserts and nights, the silence of pain and sorrow, the solitude of joy and gladness, except the Woman wrapped in silence? Who can span the bridge between the old and the new, the "converted you" and the "unconverted you," except the Blessed Virgin Mary, the bridge between the Old and New Testaments, the Jewish girl who brought forth the Messiah, Son of the Almighty?

"Near the cross of Jesus stood his mother and his mother's sister, Mary the wife of Clopas, and Mary of Magdala. Seeing his mother and the disciple he loved standing near her, Jesus said to

his mother, 'Woman, this is your son.' Then to the disciple he said, 'This is your mother.'"

— John 19:25–26 —

Even if they laugh

So many of us are afraid of ridicule. We crave the approval of our fellow men. We are afraid to "stand out from the crowd," but that is what God wants us to do, if we are to live the Gospel without compromise.

To be a Christian means to risk everything, including your life. Nothing can be held back. You may be laughed at, ridiculed, and rejected. You may be maligned, misunderstood, gossiped about, or persecuted. But you have to walk that path, following Christ's footsteps, because you love him. Yes, there is a risk in opening your heart to God and to your fellow man, but it has to be done. We must measure ourselves by Christ's own example.

"If anyone wants to be a follower of mine, let him renounce himself and take up his cross every day and follow me. For anyone who wants to save his life will lose it; but anyone who loses his life for my sake, that man will save it."

– Luke 9:23–24 –

If you really want to know

Surrender to God means opening oneself to him day after day, minute after minute, until nothing matters but his will. You say, "Lord, here I am. Speak, your servant is listening. What must I do?"

He answers, "The call of the present moment is my will for you. I want you to follow in my footsteps, wherever they lead. Do not use your own intelligence. Just follow me. Be simple, childlike, docile to my wishes. Then you will know happiness. You will know freedom. You will know me. And then I will no longer call you 'servant'; I will call you 'friend'."

"Lord, my heart is not proud, not haughty my eyes. / I have not gone after things too great, nor marvels beyond me. / Truly I have set my soul in silence and peace, / A weaned child on its mother's breast, / Even so is my soul."

– Psalm 130 (131) –

A chink...

Loneliness is something every human being has to face, for it is the hunger for perfect union. Even happily married people know loneliness, for no one can penetrate another's innermost being. Loneliness ultimately comes from not knowing God loves us, for as St. Augustine writes, "Our hearts are restless until they rest in thee."

Loneliness can be the chink through which the devil tries to destroy chastity or marital fidelity. He will try to tempt us through daydreams, through imagining the perfect partner, friend, husband or wife who will understand us completely and fill our needs. This is pure illusion, and we must be very alert. Then God will give us the graces we need, and he will fill our hearts with his own image.

"Whoever drinks this water will get thirsty again; but anyone who drinks the water that shall give will never be thirsty again: the wate

that I shall give will turn into a spring inside him, welling up to eternal life."

— John 4:13–14 —

...or an opportunity

Loneliness is present in every relationship: between husbands and wives, children and parents, and the closest of friends. It brings us to the hidden garden of our own hearts, to which God alone has access. Loneliness can be fruitful for those who follow Christ, because it can lead us to him. It can be his gift to us.

The key that opens to you the true meaning of loneliness is when you share it with Christ. He gives you his loneliness. Is there anyone who was lonelier than Christ? For God to become man was certainly lonely. If you walk into Gethsemane and spend time with him there, you will truly understand what loneliness is. When you share God's loneliness, yours and his blend together.

If you have faith, you can invite Christ into your loneliness. What I do is to invite him for a cup of tea! I take out my Bible, and I set out a cup of tea for myself and for him. This is in my imagination, of course, but that way, I can talk to him. I read from the Gospel, and something strikes me, and I say

"Do you really mean that? Do you really mean for us to love as you do? That's impossible!" He answers, "Yes, I know it's impossible, but all things are possible with me." (That answer comes from another part of the Gospel.) You see what I mean?

"Peace I bequeath you, my own peace I give you, a peace the world cannot give, this is my gift to you. Do not let your hearts be troubled or afraid."

― John 14:27 ―

A new world

Joy consists in possessing what one most greatly desires. What is it that you desire most of all at this moment? Maybe you have no joy because you desire the wrong things, the possession of which does not bring real, lasting joy?

To be truly happy is to do what God wants. Listen quietly, so that you might hear what God wishes of you. His will might appear to bring pain, but if you follow him, the pain will be accompanied by a strange joy. To give ourselves completely to God is the life of a Christian, and if we do this, we will discover joy so immense that our everyday life will be completely transformed. We will find ourselves living in a new reality.

"A woman in childbirth suffers because her time has come, but when she has given birth to the child she forgets the suffering...So it is with you you are sad now, but I shall see you again, and

your hearts will be full of joy, and that joy no one shall take from you."

~ John 16:21–22 ~

Sharing

Jesus loves us so much that he gives us the opportunity to share in his rejection. This means sharing in his crucifixion. He asks us to lift up our pain, and to lay it in his cupped hands. It then becomes like the water that is added to the wine in the sacrament of the Eucharist. The Lord takes our pain, especially the pain of rejection, and uses it to help others throughout the world. He and his Mother are at our side to help us walk in faith.

"On their way out, they came across a man from Cyrene, Simon by name, and enlisted him to carry his cross."

— Matthew 27:32 —

"'Jesus,' he said, 'remember me when you come into your kingdom.' 'Indeed, I promise you,' he replied 'today you will be with me in paradise.'

— Luke 23:42–3 —

Safe place

Whenever I feel that life is too much for me, I take refuge at the foot of the Cross. Even if it seems that the whole world is shrouded in darkness, I know, although I can neither see, hear, not understand, that I am safe at the feet of my crucified Savior.

"'Father,' he prayed, 'everything is possible for you! Take this cup away from me. But let it be as you, not I would have it.'"

– Mark 14:36 –

"Then an angel appeared to him, coming from heaven to give him strength."

– Luke 22:44 –

The touch of Jesus

In the Gospel of the Transfiguration, one line always stood out for me: "Jesus came up to them, touched them, and said, 'Stand up, do not be afraid.' And when they raised their eyes, they saw no one but Jesus."

In the awful, lonely days of my life, that was the only thing that mattered. It would seem as if he touched me. I would open my eyes filled with tears and despair, and suddenly I would see Jesus. I would get up, wash my face, and go about the work of the moment.

That's what the Gospel means to me: nourishment, strength, and the courage to keep going, no matter what the obstacles.

"I have told you all this so that you may find peace in me. In the world you will have trouble but be brave: I have conquered the world."

– John 16:33 –

Failure

How often we look at ourselves and feel we are total failures. We grow older, we look at our lives, and we don't feel there is anything worthwhile in them. That is the moment when we should go to Golgotha and look at Jesus on the Cross. There is no greater failure than Jesus Christ. In fact, he was the "perfect failure."

"Unless a wheat grain falls on the ground and dies, it remains only a single grain, but if it dies, it yields a rich harvest."

‒ John 12:24 ‒

Ground zero

Sometimes in the course of life, you watch what seemed to be God's will for you crumble into nothing. And you can't do anything about it but watch.

This happened to me. I knew dimly at that time what I see more clearly today: this was the moment when God really picked me up and said, "Now I am offering you the union with me that you seek. The other side of my cross is empty. Come, be nailed upon it. This is our marriage bed."

All I could answer was, "Help me, Lord. I don't have the courage to climb on the cross."

"Do not let your hearts be troubled. Trust in God still, and trust in me. I shall return to take you with me so that where I am, you may be too. You know the way to the place where I am going."

~ John 13:1–3 ~

A new angle on sin

We are all sinners, but let us never forget that we are saved sinners. It is obvious that we are going to stumble a million times between birth and death, but when we look at the Gospel, we see immediately that God came, not for the perfect ones, but for sinners. That means, for each of us.

But don't let sin twist you. Don't let the Seducer make you feel that because you've sinned, you are cut off from God. Tell him, "Go back to hell where you belong, Satan, and stay there!" Confess, "I have sinned. I'm sorry. Lord, have mercy on me." Then listen to the devil sizzle as he goes down! The moment you say, "Lord, have mercy," the devil disappears.

If we say we have no sin in us, we are deceiving ourselves and refusing to admit the truth, but if we acknowledge our sins, then God who is faithful and just will forgive us our sins and purify us from everything that is wrong."

— 1 John 1:8–9 —

Consolation

We who suffer, we who are in anguish and anxiety, should stand with the Virgin Mary under the cross. Through her, we will find the courage to keep believing, and the strength to bear the burdens that tear our souls apart.

How did Our Lady bear the passion of Christ? She was present on the way of the cross. She watched him fall; she saw him being beaten; she saw the face that was so dear to her covered with mud and dust. As Simeon had predicted at the time of the Presentation in the Temple, she felt the sword piercing her own heart. She and her Son were always united. What he felt, she felt, for she was his mother.

We have a Mother who understands Before he died, Jesus handed her to John, the beloved disciple, as his Mother and ours. I we turn to her, she will show us how to sor things out in the silence of our hearts. Sh will help us to grow in faith and love, and t follow her Son, as she did. She will lead u to his resurrection.

The Virgin Mary, the one through whom God came to us, will lead us back to him.

"'I am the handmaid of the Lord,' said Mary, 'let what you have said be done to me.'"

— Luke 1:38 —

360-degree turn

Repentance is not the same thing as remorse or self-condemnation—"Oh, what a fool I've been!" It is more than contrition and admitting one's mistakes. No, repentance is a moral and spiritual revolution within our souls.

To repent is not just acknowledging that I have done wrong. It means turning my back on the sin, turning in a new direction, and beginning again to try to incarnate the Gospel with my life.

Repentance implies the breaking down of pride, self-assurance, and the innermost citadels of our self-will. To truly repent is one of the hardest things in life, but it is basic to all spiritual growth.

On this hinges the future of Christianity for if I do not begin to incarnate Christ's teachings, how can the world believe in him'

"They all complained, 'He has gone to stay at a sinner's house.' But Zacchaeus stood his groun

and said to the Lord, 'Look, sir, I am going to give half my property to the poor, and if I have cheated anybody I will pay him back four times the amount.' And Jesus said to him, 'Today salvation has come to this house.'"

– Luke 19:7–10 –

And let it go

Be at peace. No matter what guilt there may have been, he has risen, and his blood has washed it away. You can come to him and make a cup of your hands, and one drop of his blood will cleanse you, if you have faith in his mercy and say, "Lord, forgive me."

A Christian can have sorrow—a gentle sorrow, and a prayer that he not commit the same sin as before. But lingering guilt should be totally absent in one who has faith in God's mercy. Let us pray for the simplicity of a child who has just broken Mama's favorite cup and who runs into her arms, crying, "I'm sorry!"

Let go of your guilt. Set your doubts aside. Put all that in a sort of bundle and throw it out! We are Christians and we live by faith. It is as if hail were falling on the roof, but inside we are warm and cozy, for in our hearts is a flame, and in our souls, a love stronger than death. We believe, and nothing that happens to us can destroy that faith Christ is in our midst, and our Advocate, the

Helper of the Poor, is by our side. What have we to fear?

"I tell you, there will be more rejoicing in heaven over one repentant sinner than over ninety-nine men who have no need of repentance."

— Luke 15:7 —

Healing

The pity of God is immense and profound. It is like a fresh wind that comes up suddenly on a torrid day. It is like a cool evening, when the sky is pink and blue and red, and beautiful to behold. It is as gentle as a loving mother rocking a cradle. It is like oil that softens the heart.

If we let God's pity penetrate the deepest levels of our being, so many painful things will disappear. If we allow the gentleness of Christ to take hold of us, so many of our inner hurts, fears and negative emotions can be assuaged. We will find our depression lifting, for it is Christ himself who visits the very depths of our heart. Having lifted up the crushed and bruised soul, he embraces the whole person, and speaks words of tender affection. Even sin can be burned up in this pity, for God loves sinners.

If we enter into the divine pity, we will ourselves be able to extend it towards others, embracing them, holding them, and calling them "Brother, sister, friend."

"A leper came to him and pleaded on his knees: 'If you want to,' he said, 'you can cure me.' Feeling sorry for him, Jesus stretched out his hand and touched him. 'Of course I want to!' he said. 'Be cured.'"

— Matthew 8:2–3 —

Love song

Long ago, an ordinary man called John laid his head on the breast of Christ, and listened to the heartbeats of the Lord. Who can guess what that man felt as he heard the beat of that mighty heart? None of us will ever be in his place, but all of us can hear, if we listen, the song of love God sings to us. If we meditate on the most holy sacrament of the Eucharist, we will hear, not only his heartbeats, but our own hearts beating in unison with his. We will be united with our Lord and our God.

God's heart is our only true resting place, the oasis to which he calls us. The key to his heart is identification with all his little ones, a deep love that requires so great an enlargement of heart that we cannot even aspire to it unless God shows us the way.

Let us pray for that enlargement of heart.

"I give you a new commandment: love one another; just as I have loved you, you also mu

love one another. By this love you have for one another, everyone will know you are my disciples."

— John 13:34–35 —

The warmth of God's mercy

Do you feel the warmth of God's mercy? Do you feel the tenderness that embraces you? Do you feel the knock at your heart that says, "You needn't be lonely and worried about this matter; I am with you. I am in you." Do you feel his consolation—not emotionally, but spiritually, in faith? Do you feel the touch of his hand upon your heart, healing the wounds of sin?

"I am the good shepherd; I know my own and my own know me, just as the Father knows me and I know the Father; and I lay down my life for my sheep."

— John 10:14–15 —

Who is Catherine?

- A daughter of Russia, who brought the spiritual traditions of her native land to the Western Church.

- A laywoman, who taught that daily life, no matter what the circumstances, can be filled with glory and become a road to sanctity.

- A believer whose faith-vision embraced all aspects of human life.

- A woman passionately in love with God, who saw his face in every human being.

Burning with faith, she challenged the Christian conscience of her day, living the Gospel radically in the face of communism, economic and racial injustice, secularization and apathy.

Born in 1896 to an aristocratic family, Catherine Kolyschkine grew up in the Ukraine, Egypt, and Paris. Married at 15 to Boris de Hueck, she served as a nurse in the

First World War. The couple fled Russia in 1918, barely escaping death at the hands of the Bolsheviks. Eventually they settled in Canada.

Baptized in the Orthodox Church, she was raised by parents with a deep, incarnated faith and an openness to other religious traditions. When she came to England in 1921, she became a Catholic.

Wealthy in Russia, she experienced the grinding poverty of the immigrant in the New World. When her economic situation improved, she was pursued by the call of Christ to renounce everything to follow him. With the blessing of her bishop, she went to live a life of prayer and simple service to the poor in the slums of Toronto.

Her example of radical Gospel living became a magnet for men and women in search of a way to live their faith. Answering their need, she became the foundress of Friendship House in Toronto and Harlem then of the Madonna House community.

A foreigner, whose mentality was different from those with whom she worked whose breadth of vision was a constant challenge to those who wanted a "comfortable religion," Catherine was often misunder stood, rejected, and persecuted. Though her human suffering was great, it united her to the crucified Lord she longed to follow, and to all her brothers and sisters.

Her second marriage in 1943 to the American journalist Eddie Doherty ignited new conflicts in Friendship House. Catherine resigned as director, and she and Eddie retired to the little village of Combermere, in Ontario, Canada.

What seemed like the end of the road turned out to be the most fruitful period of Catherine's life. The community of Madonna House was born, and grew into an open family of laymen, laywomen, and priests, living in love and breathing from the "two lungs," East and West, of the Catholic Church. In its way of life are the seeds of a new Christian civilization.

Catherine de Hueck Doherty died in Combermere on December 14, 1985 after a long illness. She was undoubtedly one of the great Christians of our time.

The excerpts used in this book are taken from the following books published by Madonna House Publications:

Dearly Beloved, Volumes I & III

Dear Parents

Donkey Bells

Grace in Every Season

Kiss of Christ

To find out about the progress of Catherine Doherty's cause for canonization in the Catholic Church, please visit the web site:

www.catherinedoherty.org

To learn more about the life and work of the world-wide Madonna House Apostolate founded by Catherine Doherty, please visit:

www.madonnahouse.org